The HAIR ALPHABET with Lady T

Taylor Asianeigh Bazile

MILTON & HUGO L.L.C.
4407 Park Ave., Suite 5
Union City, NJ 07087, USA

Website: www. miltonandhugo.com
Hotline: 1- 888-778-0033
Email: info@miltonandhugo.com

Ordering Information:
Quantity sales. Special discounts are available on quantity purchases by corporations, associations, and others. For details, contact the publisher at the address above.

ISBN-13:   979-8-89285-312-5   [Paperback Edition]
              979-8-89285-311-8   [Hardback Edition]
              979-8-89285-310-1   [Digital Edition]

Rev. date: 11/24/2025

The HAIR ALPHABET with Lady T

Taylor Asianeigh Bazile

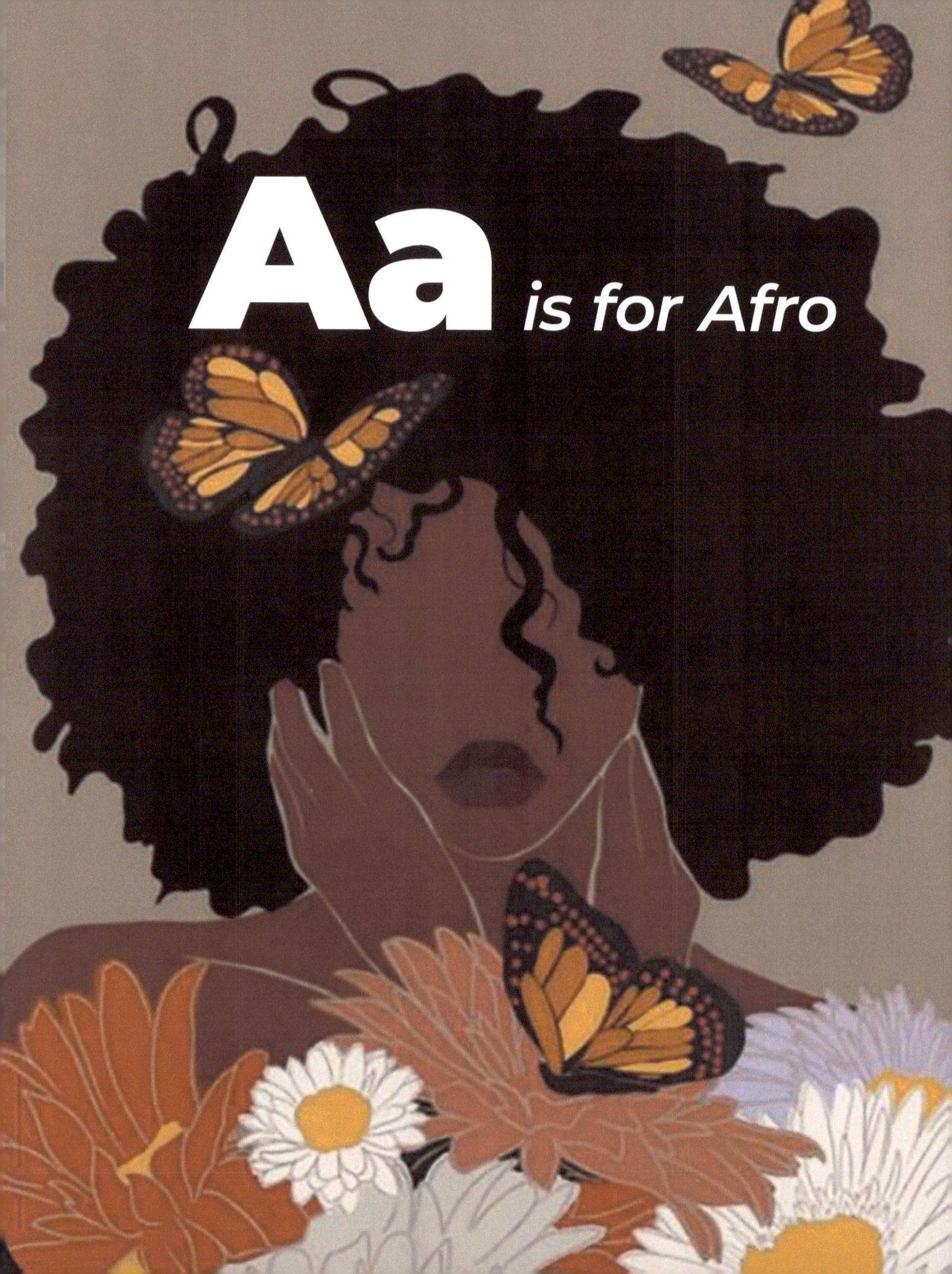

Aa *is for Afro*

Bb is Braids

Cc is for Crown

Dd *is for Dreads*

Ee *is for Edge*

Ff is for Flat Iron

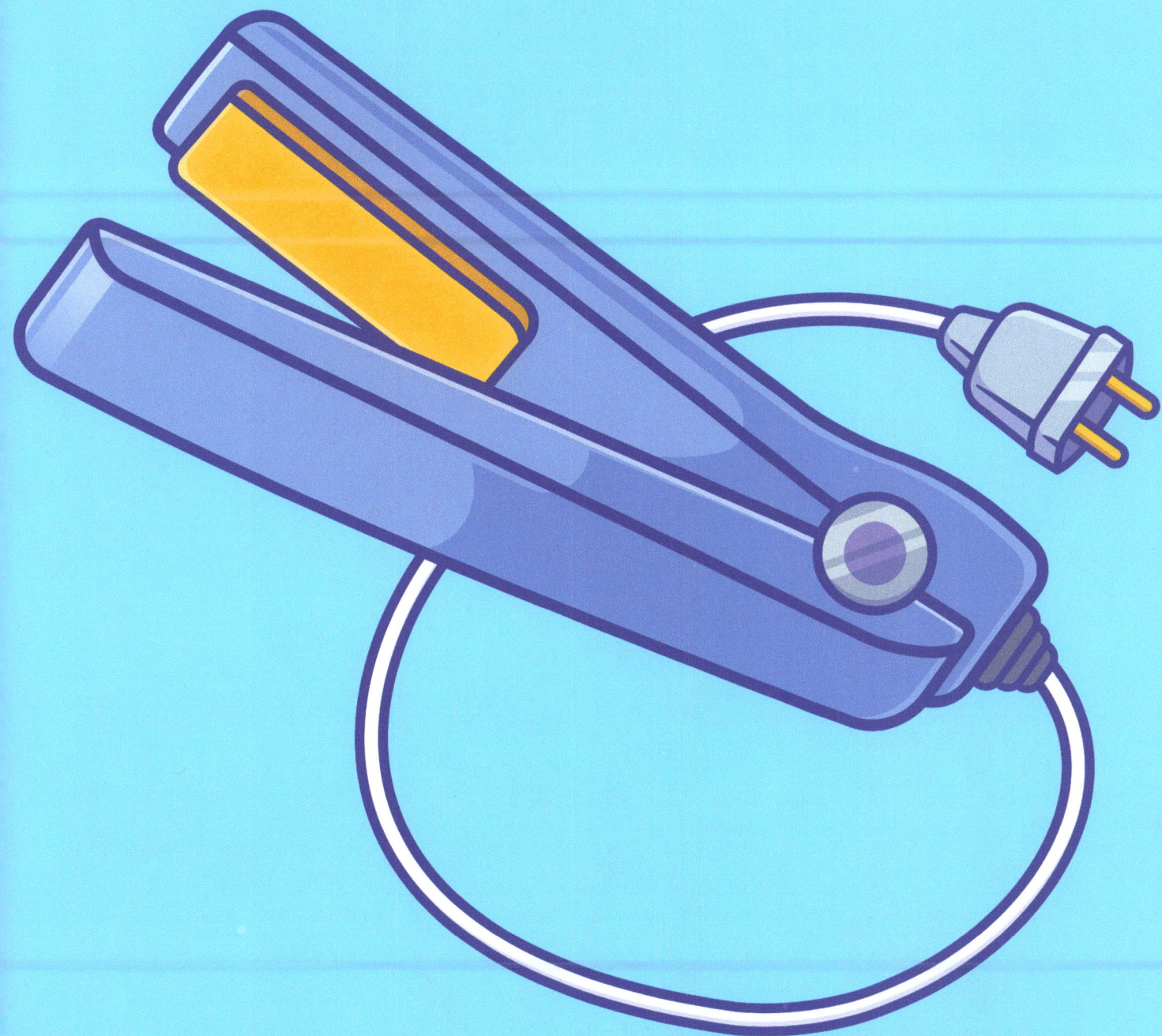

Gg is for Gel

Hh *is for Hot Comb*

Ii is for Innovative

Jj

is for Jheri Curl

Kk

is for Knotless Braids

Ll is for Locs

Mm

is for Moisturizer

Nn

is for Natural Hair

Oo

is for Optimistic Growth

Pp is for Perm

Qq *is for Queen*

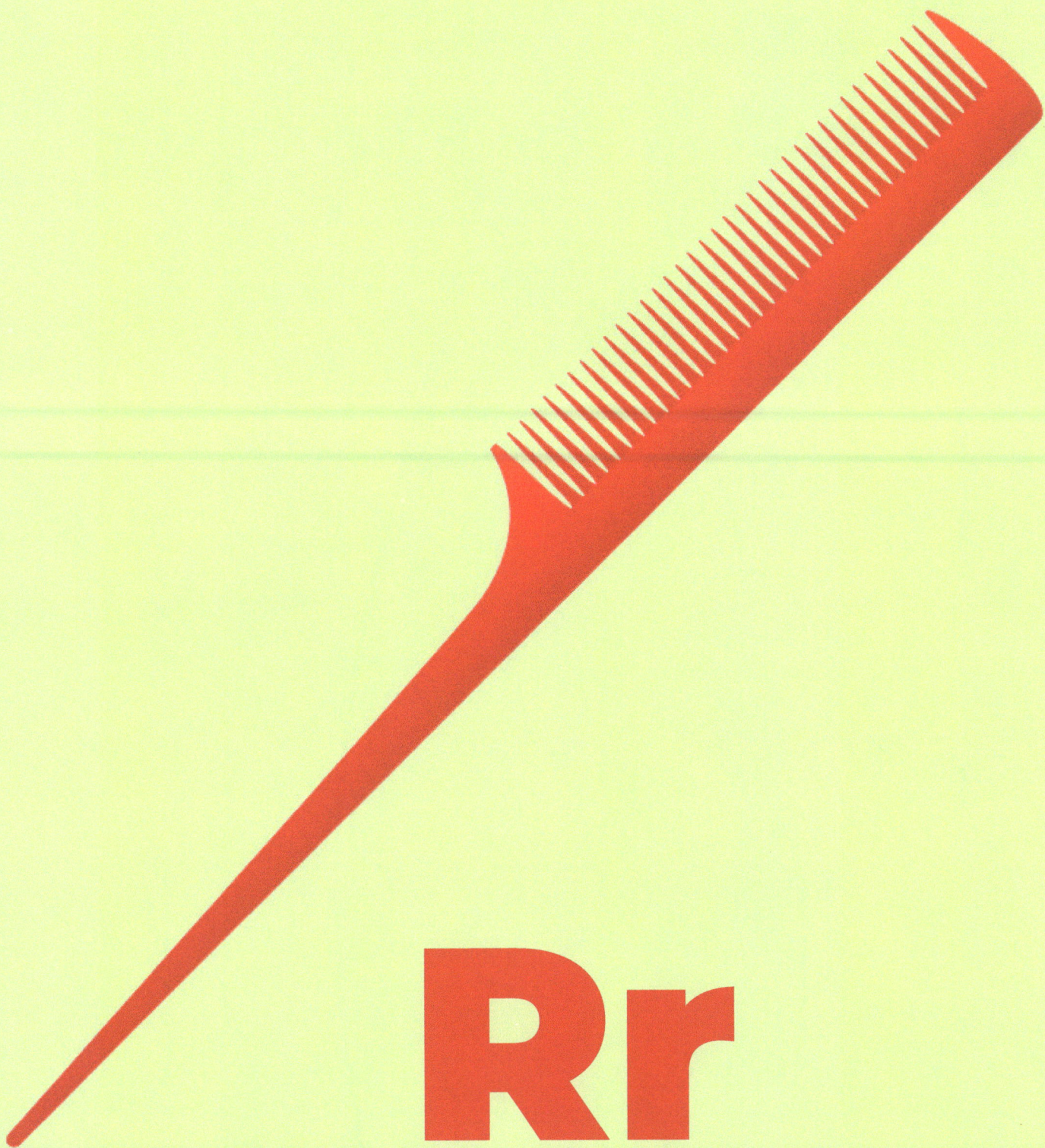

Rr

is for Rattail

Ss is for Shampoo

Tt is for Twists

Uu *is for Unique*

Vv *is for Volume*

Ww *is Wigs*

Xx *is Xtraordinary*

Yy

is for Youthful

Zz

is for Zealous